Contents

What is bullying?   4

Making excuses   6

Who bullies?   8

Where does it happen?   10

How does it feel?   12

Why are some people bullied?   14

Why do people become bullies?   16

How do you stop a bully?   18

What will happen?   20

What if you don't tell?   22

Bullies need help too   24

Feeling good   26

Being friends   28

Words to remember   30

Organisations, helplines and websites   31

Index   32

What is bullying?

Hurting someone by punching or kicking them is bullying. So is calling someone names or saying unkind things to hurt their feelings. Making someone feel **lonely** and left out is bullying too.

When Declan first came to his new school, some children bullied him because he is from Ireland.

Talking About

Bullying

Nicola Edwards

First published in the UK in 2003 by
Chrysalis Children's Books
An imprint of Chrysalis Books Group Plc
The Chrysalis Building
Bramley Road
London W10 6SP

Paperback edition first published in 2005

ISBN 184138 824 6 (hb)
ISBN 184458 313 9 (pb)

British Library Cataloguing in Publication Data for this book is available from the British Library.

Editorial manager: Joyce Bentley
Senior editor: Sarah Nunn
Picture researchers: Terry Forshaw, Lois Charlton
Designer: Wladek Szechter
Editor: Kate Phelps
Consultant: Dr Ute Navidi, Head of Policy, ChildLine

Printed in China

The pictures used in this book do not show the actual people named in the the text.

Foreword

Calling someone names, shutting someone out from groups of friends, stealing their possessions or money or attacking them physically are just some of the acts of bullying that blight the lives of many children. If not tackled in early childhood, bullying can have desperate and devastating effects and carry over into adult lives.

Through real-live scenarios set in and out of school, **Talking About Bullying** helps parents, carers and teachers listen and look out for the signs of bullying. It helps children talk about what is happening to them and suggests ways of stopping bullying behaviour. Explaining why some children become bullies and need help with this issue, the book takes a no-blame approach to bullying. Like other titles in the **Talking About series**, it encourages children to identify someone who will listen to them – a trusted adult, a friend of their own age or ChildLine – so taking the first step towards finding help.

Informative and thought-provoking, the **Talking About** series tackles some disturbing aspects of contemporary society: bullying, divorce, domestic violence, racism and eating problems. Adults often try to protect children from these problems or believe they will not understand. Taking children through a series of situations they can identify with – using words and images – also means offering alternative ways of resolving conflict. Each book shows that even very young children are not passive observers or victims but want to make sense of their world and act to make life better for themselves, their families and other children.

Ute Navidi, Head of Policy, ChildLine

These bullies were nasty to Anita because she wore glasses and always did well in exams.

Bullying is also taking or breaking something belonging to someone else. Bullying happens a lot. It's a problem for many people.

Making excuses

Bullies often say they are only **teasing** or having a bit of fun. They may say they don't mean any harm.

William tried to say he was only joking when the teacher noticed he was being a bully.

Clare felt very
sad and lonely when she
was bullied.

It's not your fault if you
are being bullied.

But being bullied is never any fun.
Bullying often makes people very frightened
and unhappy. It is always wrong.

Who bullies?

Girls and boys can be bullies. Sometimes a bully is the leader of a **gang** and bosses people around. This makes a bully feel important.

A gang of girls bullied Mary and said unkind things about her behind her back.

Martin was bullied
by Joe and forced to give
his pocket money to him.

Some bullies act alone or
in pairs. They like to make
other people afraid of them.

Adults can be
bullies, too –
at work or
even at home.

Where does it happen?

Rani dreaded lunchtimes at school. Bullies teased her because of her size.

Children often bully others when adults cannot see what they are doing. Bullies are **cowards** – they don't want people to tell them off or punish them.

Bullies took Emily's packed lunch
away from her on the way to school.

Bullying sometimes happens while children
are on their way to school or going home.
Some bullies pick on children in the
playground at break or lunchtime.

How does it feel?

Being bullied can make people feel very sad and scared. Some children feel **confused**. They don't understand why a bully is picking on them.

Lucy felt **ashamed** when bullies tore her clothes. She didn't want to tell her mum and upset her.

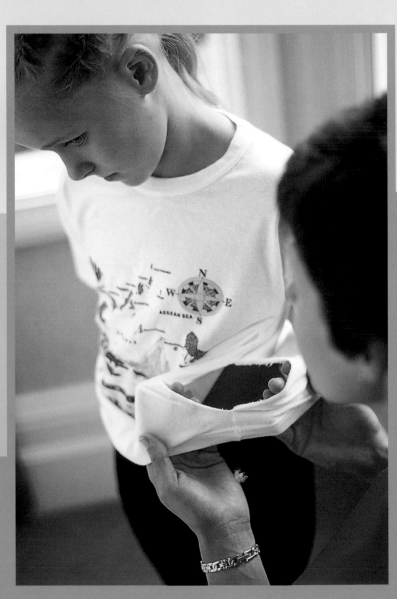

Ben felt sick every morning before school.
He was being bullied by a boy in his class.

Bullying makes people feel bad about themselves. They may be afraid that there is no **escape** from the bullying.

Bullied children often feel lonely. You can help them by being their friend.

Why are some people bullied?

Bullies tend to pick on people they see as being different in some way. This might be because of how someone looks or speaks or acts.

Sometimes bullies try to make children feel bad about doing well at school.

These girls bullied Nelupa because her family came from Bangladesh.

Bullies like to feel **powerful**. They feel good if they have upset someone or made them feel afraid.

Why do people become bullies?

Bullies try to make themselves feel good by making others feel bad.

It makes children feel big when they bully people in front of others.

Jack picked on people at school because he was bullied at home by his older brother.

Bullies are often **jealous** of the person they are bullying.

Bullies might be feeling angry or sad about something and want other people to know how it feels.

How do you stop a bully?

If someone is being bullied, it is very important that they tell an adult they **trust** about what is happening.

Gina told her teacher that she was being bullied.

Mario felt better
when he told his mum he was sad
about being bullied.

Never try to fight a bully – there are
other ways of standing up for yourself.

Telling someone at home or at school about bullying
is not telling tales. People know that bullying
happens and have ways of stopping it.

19

What will happen?

Children often worry that if they tell a teacher about being bullied, the bully will find out and make things worse for them.

Dean's head teacher spoke to him in front of his parents. She asked him to imagine how it feels to be bullied. Dean said he was sorry.

Dean's teacher watched him closely to make sure that he stopped being a bully.

But teachers won't tell bullies how they know about their **behaviour**.

What if you don't tell?

Some children who are being bullied are too **worried** or scared to tell anyone. They just hope the problem will go away. But this only makes things worse.

Fiona's mum could tell she was worried about something.

When Nina was bullied
she didn't tell anyone. Then she saw the same
bully picking on someone else.

If you see someone being
bullied, tell an adult.

Bullies rely on people keeping quiet about their
behaviour. It lets them get away with it.

Bullies need help too

People who bully others are usually unhappy. Bullies often have problems or worries of their own.

Danny told his teacher that he had bullied someone when he was hurt that his mum forgot to send him a birthday card.

Oonagh said sorry to Emily for bullying her and gave her back the packed lunch she had taken.

Bullies need help to sort out their problems. This doesn't mean that there is any excuse for bullying. It is always wrong to bully someone.

Feeling good

Bullies like to feel powerful and make people feel afraid. They are unlikely to pick on people who look **confident** and happy.

Carl wasn't picked on by bullies. He always looked confident.

Joining in sports and other activities helps people to feel good and grow more confident.

Think about what makes you special.

People who feel good about themselves and feel able to stand up to a bully are less likely to be bullied.

Being *friends*

Good friends enjoy spending time together. They care about each other.

Joining in and having fun makes people feel happy.

Friends are very important. They are fun and help you when you have a problem.

Bullies may seem to have a big group of friends. But real friends stick together because they like each other, not because one is afraid of the other.

The happier you are, the easier it is to make friends – and the harder it will be for someone to bully you.

Words to remember

ashamed Feeling bad, as if you have done something wrong.

behaviour The way a person acts.

confident Feeling as if you can do anything.

confused Feeling uncertain and mixed-up.

coward Someone who acts as if they are brave when they are in a crowd but who is easily afraid when on their own.

escape A way out or a solution to a problem.

gang A group of people.

jealous Feeling that you want what someone else has got.

lonely Feeling sad, as if you have no friends.

powerful Strong and in charge.

teasing Upsetting or annoying someone just for fun.

trust Feeling that someone won't let you down.

worried Feeling bothered and unhappy about a problem.

Organisations, helplines and websites

FOR CHILDREN:

Anti-Bullying Network
Gives teachers, parents and children the opportunity to share ideas about how bullying should be tackled.
Moray House
Institute of Education
University of Edinburgh
Holyrood Road
Edinburgh EH8 8AQ
www.antibullying.net

Bullying Online
Offers support and advice to children, parents, teachers and youth leaders.
Help for bullies and their parents too.
www.bullying.co.uk

ChildLine
A charity offering information, help and advice to any child with worries or problems.
Address for adults:
45 Folgate Street, London E1 6GL
Address for children:
Freepost NATN1111, London E1 6BR
Free and confidential helpline for children and young people: 0800 1111
ChildLine Scotland bullying helpline:
0800 441111
www.childline.org.uk

Children's Legal Centre
Publishes **Bullying: a Guide to the Law – How to tackle bullying from inside and outside school.**
Advice line: 01206 873820
www.childrenslegalcentre.com

CURB (Children Under Risk of Bullying)
24-hour helpline offering support and advice:
02920 611300

Department for Education and Skills
Publishes **Bullying: Don't Suffer in Silence. An Anti-Bullying Pack for Schools (HMSO).**
www.dfes.gov.uk/bullying

Kidscape
A charity working towards preventing bullying and protecting children, Kidscape offers support, information and advice aimed at children, parents and professionals.
2 Grosvenor Gardens
London SW1W 0DH
www.kidscape.org.uk

FOR PARENTS:

Parentline Plus
Offers help, support and information to anyone parenting a child.
Helpline: 0808 800 2222
www.parentlineplus.org.uk

Young Minds
Provides information and advice to anyone concerned about the mental health of a child or young person.
Advice line: 0800 018 2138
www.youngminds.org.uk

The publishers would like to point out that they are not responsible for the content of any of the websites featured on this page.

Index

adults 9, 10, 18, 23
angry 17
ashamed 12, 30

Bangladesh 15
behaviour 21, 23, 30
boys 8
brothers 17

confident 26, 27, 30
confused 12
cowards 10, 30

exams 5

friends 13, 28, 29

gangs 8, 30
girls 8
glasses 5

happy 26, 28

Ireland 4

jealous 17, 30

kicking 4

lonely 4, 7, 13, 30

mums 12, 19, 22, 24

parents 20, 31
pocket money 9
powerful 15, 26, 30
problems 22, 24, 25, 30, 31
punching 4

sad 12, 17, 19
school 4, 10, 11, 13, 14, 17, 19
sports 27

teachers 6, 18, 20, 21, 24, 31
teasing 6, 30

worries 22, 24, 30, 31